Double Stops

for Cello

by:

Rick Mooney

Alfred Music
P.O. Box 10003
Van Nuys, CA 91410-0003
alfred.com

Copyright © 1995 by Summy-Birchard Music, division of Summy-Birchard Inc.
Exclusive print rights administered by Alfred Music
All rights reserved. Produced in USA.

ISBN-10: 0-87487-761-X
ISBN-13: 978-0-87487-761-8

T0019051

Introduction

Double stops are an excellent learning tool. In practicing them, many important skills can be developed:

- Intonation and ear training are enhanced when one pitch must be tuned against another — even if one of the notes is just an open string.

- The correct shape of the left hand and proper spacing of the fingers is developed.

- A good extended hand position is especially crucial when playing double stops.

- Certain important exceptions to a normal hand position are also learned, as with fifths and chords.

- Many passages in the cello repertoire depend upon double stop patterns in the left hand even if the bow is playing one note at a time.

In my opinion, the study of double stops should be an important part of a daily practice routine.

The problem is that most double stop exercises are too advanced for many students. This book specifically addresses that problem. "Double Stops for Cello" consists of familiar and tuneful melodies. Besides making the pieces fun to play, the fact that the songs are so recognizable helps students to know when they are playing in tune. The first folk songs are very simple, being composed of fingered notes against open strings. The book then progresses through closed fingering patterns, extensions, shifting, sixths, thirds, etc. The pieces are placed in order of difficulty except for the bowing studies at the back of the book which should be brought out and used as needed.

I would like to thank my friends and their students for trying out the preliminary versions of this book and giving me their valuable comments. Also, special thanks to Lynn and Haide for their assistance in acquiring source materials.

I hope you find this book as fun and useful as I have. Enjoy!

Rick Mooney

Contents

Go Tell Aunt Rhody

United States

Long Long Ago

Thomas H. Bayly

Three Blind Mice

England

Twinkle, Twinkle Little Star
(Ah! Vous dirai-je Maman)

France

Amazing Grace

United States

Lightly Row
(Hänschen Klein)

Germany

Note: Also play in the key of G

Lullaby

Wales

Boil Them Cabbage Down

United States

Skip to My Lou

United States

Ten Little Indians

United States

The Mulberry Bush

England

This Old Man

England

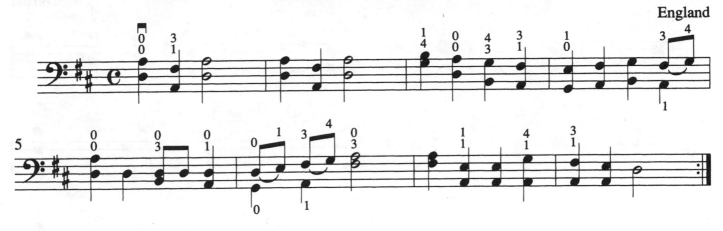

Camptown Races

Stephen C. Foster

Auld Lang Syne

Scotland

Polly Wolly Doodle

United States

Berceuse

Franz Schubert

Mary had a Little Lamb

Sara J. Hale

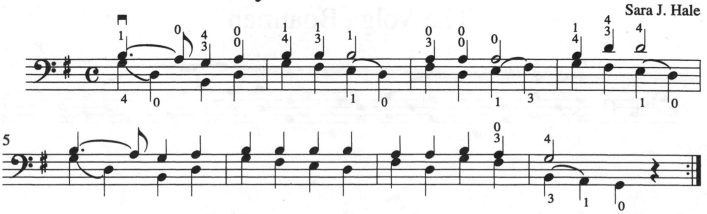

Cockles and Mussels

Ireland

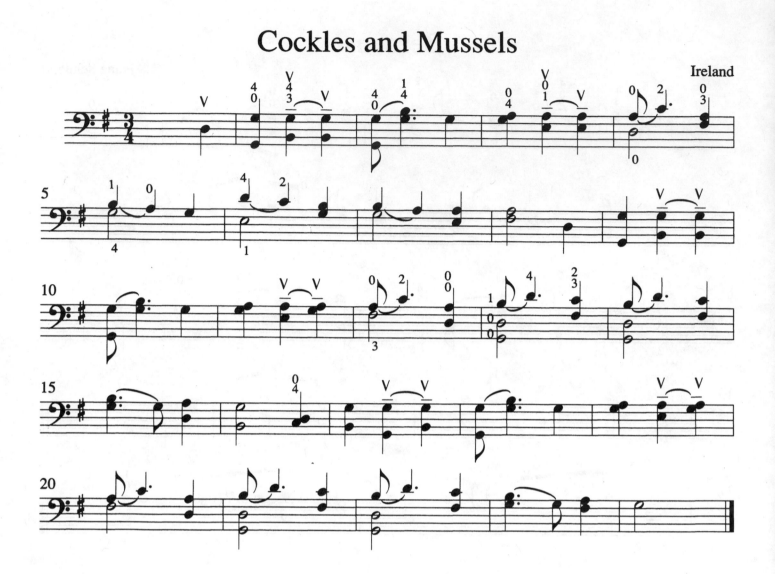

The Volga Boatmen

Russia

Sur le Pont d'Avignon

France

Home on the Range

United States

[13]

Clair de Lune

France

When Johnny Comes Marching Home

Patrick S. Gilmore
(Louis Lambert)

Drunken Sailor

Sea Shanty

Highland Lad

Scotland

Old MacDonald

United States

Happy Birthday To You

Mildred and Patty Hill

Fuchs, du hast die Gans Gestohlen
(Song of the Wind)

Germany

Blow the Man Down

Sea Chanty

Yankee Doodle

United States

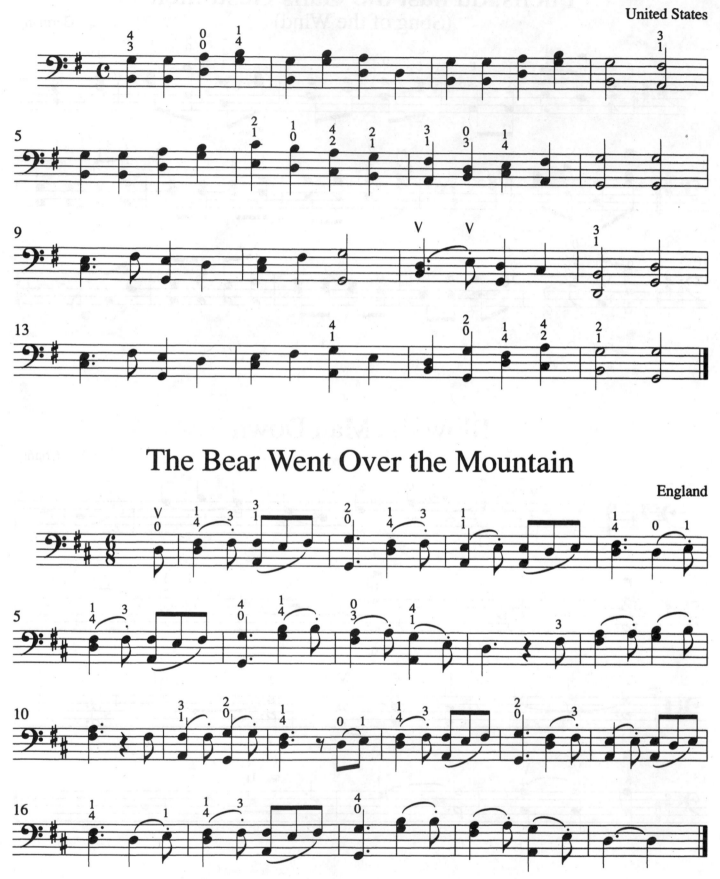

The Bear Went Over the Mountain

England

Coventry Carol

England

Greensleeves

England

poco rit.

[19]

The Blue Bells of Scotland

Scotland

Oh Susannah

Stephen C. Foster

Streets of Laredo
(The Cowboy's Lament)

United States

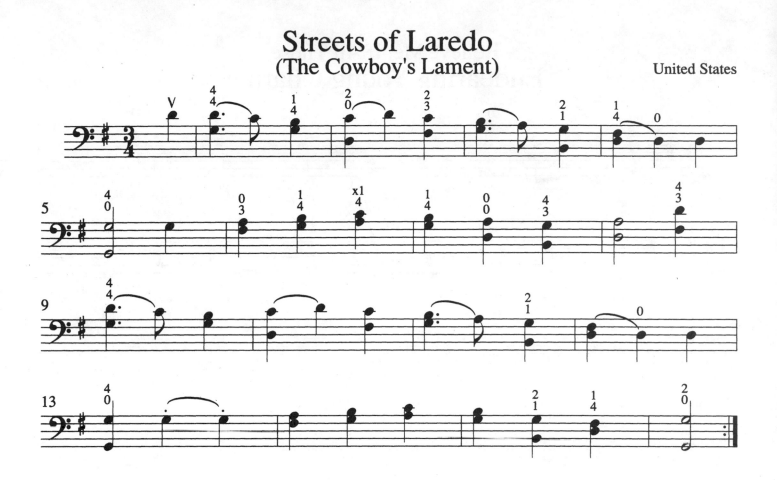

Clementine

United States

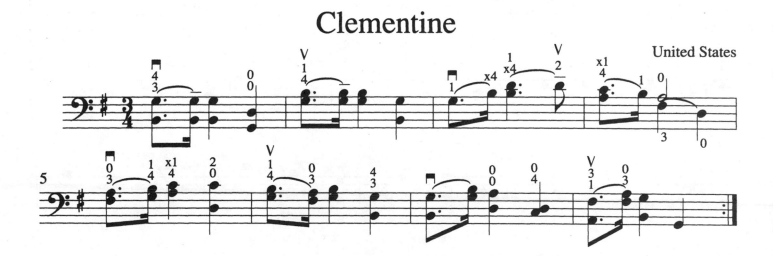

Believe Me, If All Those
Endearing Young Charms

Ireland

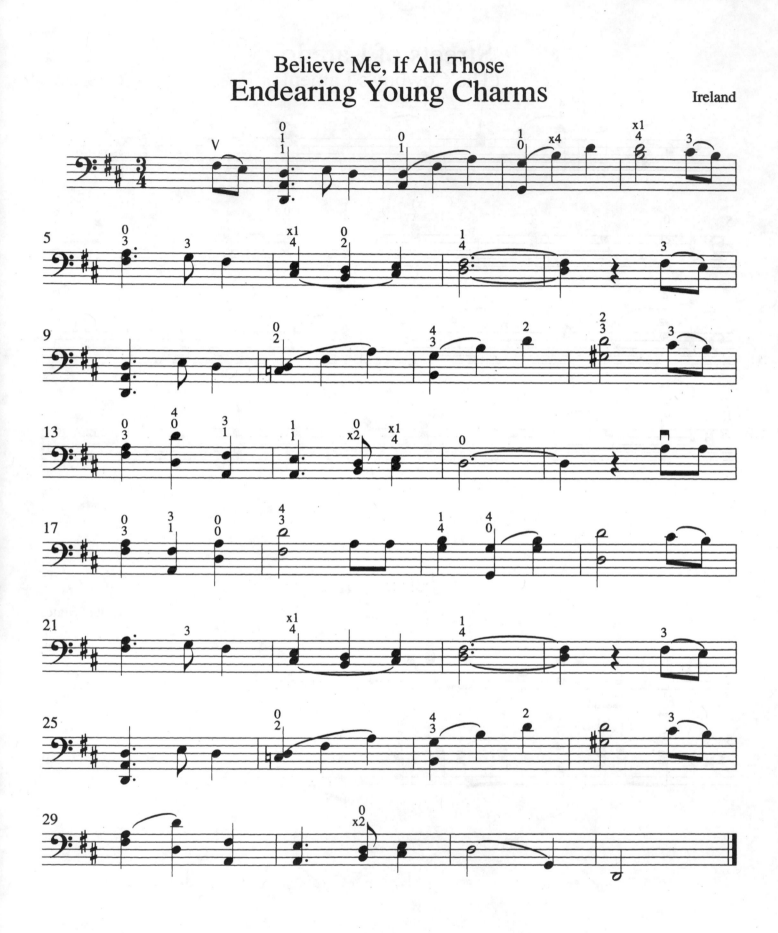

America, the Beautiful

Samuel A. Ward

Sweet Betsy from Pike

United States

Aura Lee

Ode to Joy

Ludwig van Beethoven

London Bridge is Falling Down

England

Soldier's March

Robert Schumann

French Folk Song

France

When the Saints Go Marching In

United States

Swing Low, Sweet Chariot

United States

Note: Try swinging the eighth notes

Fine

D. C. al Fine

My Bonnie

H. J. Fuller

Get Along Little Doggies

United States

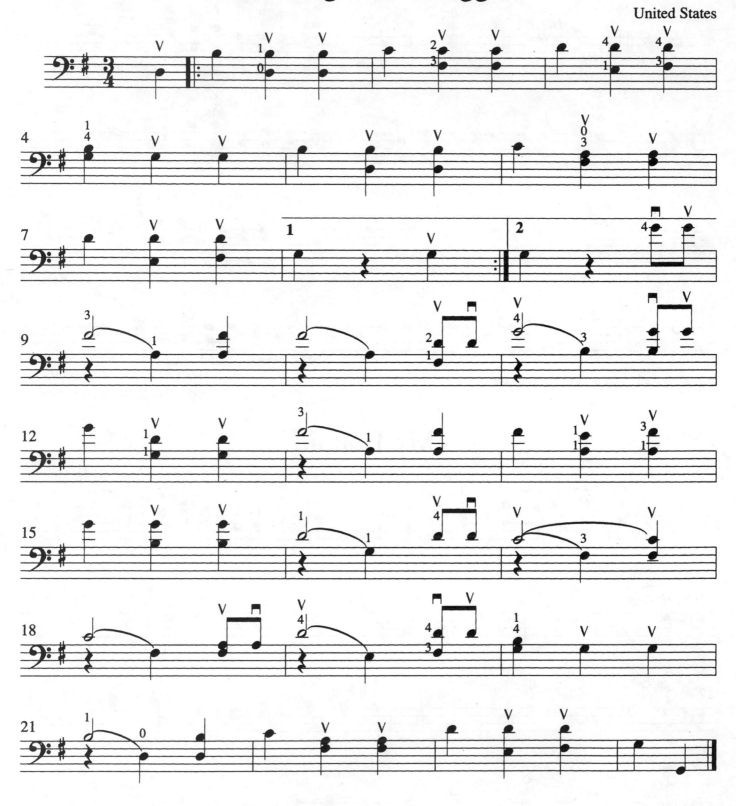

Londonderry Air
(Danny Boy)

Ireland

The Old Gray Mare

United States

The Ash Grove

Wales

Pop Goes the Weasel

England

The Farmer in the Dell

England

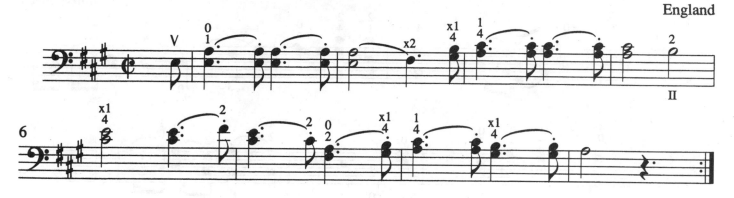

Chopsticks

Unknown

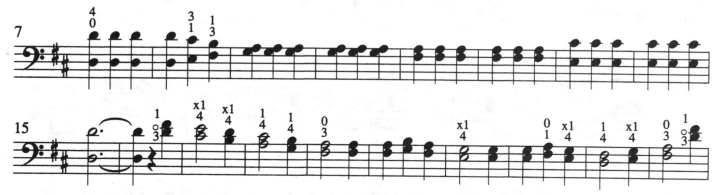

I've Been Working on the Railroad

United States

Rigadoon

Henry Purcell

French Folk Song in Sixths

Preparation for Lee Exercise

Lee Exercise

Sebastian Lee

Twinkle in B-Flat Major

Bowing Variations:

Twinkle with Chords

Bowing Variations:

Alphabetical Index